W9-ATY-439

C. S. Lewis

My Favorite Writer

Megan Lappi

WEIGL PUBLISHERS INC.

C. S. Lewis

MILESTONES

1898 Born in Belfast, Northern Ireland, on November 29

1917 Volunteers for military service in World War I

1919 Publishes first book, *Spirits in Bondage,* a book of poetry

1923 Graduates from Oxford University with an English degree

1938 *Out of the Silent Planet,* a space novel, is published

1950 *The Lion, the Witch and the* **Wardrobe** is published

1956 Marries Joy Greshem and wins the Dale Carnegie Award

1960 Joy dies of cancer

1963 Dies on November 22

As a child, Clive Staples (C. S.) Lewis loved stories. With his brother Warren, he wrote stories about a place called "Animal Land." Clive was imaginative, even as an adult. He always knew that one day he would write something important.

Clive spent most of his adult life teaching at Oxford University and writing books for adults. While there, he met John Ronald Reuel Tolkien, who wrote *The Lord of the Rings*. Both writers liked stories about people and animals living in **mythical**, far-off lands.

Clive did not begin writing books for children until later in his life. He is best known for writing The Chronicles of Narnia. The Chronicles of Narnia series began with *The Lion, the Witch and the Wardrobe*. Clive wrote the seven Narnia books between 1950 and 1956. Although children asked if he would write more books in the series, Clive decided that he would not. He thought it was best to stop writing while his fans still wanted more.

Early Childhood

"(I am) the product of long corridors, empty sunlit rooms, upstairs indoor silences, attics explored in solitude, distant noises of gurgling cisterns and pipes, and the noise of wind under the tiles."
C. S. Lewis

Clive Staples Lewis was born on November 29, 1898, in Belfast, Northern Ireland. His father, Albert Lewis, was a lawyer. Albert liked to write poetry, but his work was never published. Clive's mother, Flora, studied mathematics at university. It was unusual for women to attend university in the nineteenth century. Flora and Albert had two sons, Warren and Clive. The two boys were born nearly 3 years apart. Flora stayed home to raise the boys.

Clive was a very opinionated little boy. When he was 4 years old, he announced to his family that he wanted to be called "Jacksie." His family called him Jacksie. Eventually, the name was shortened to "Jack." His family and friends called him Jack for the rest of his life.

Warren and Jack were friends. A **governess** cared for the boys in the morning. In the afternoon, they played by themselves.

Londonderry

BELFAST

IRELAND

Galway

Dublin ★

Limerick

Waterford

Cork

N
W E
S

| 0 | 10 | 20 | 30 | MILES |
| 0 | 16 | 32 | 48 | KILOMETERS |

Belfast is Northern Ireland's capital city. About 350,000 people live in Belfast.

In 1905, the Lewis family moved to a new house outside of Belfast. "Little Lea" was a three-story brick house. It had a large attic in which the boys liked to play. Warren and Jack spent many hours in the attic playing hide-and-seek and writing stories about Animal Land.

Soon after they moved to Little Lea, Warren was sent to boarding school in Great Britain. The two boys were used to spending most of their time together. They found it difficult to be apart. Jack's life was different with Warren away at school. Jack read many books. In the evenings, Jack and his mother usually read together until it was time for him to go to bed. He especially liked Beatrix Potter's books.

■ Like Jack's mother, many mothers read fairy tales to their children.

Growing Up

Jack hated the school. He begged his father to send him somewhere—anywhere—else.

In 1908, Jack's mother died of cancer. Her death was especially difficult for Albert, who was left with two young boys to raise on his own. Albert decided to send Jack to boarding school with Warren, even though Jack was only 9 years old.

Jack hated the school. He begged his father to send him somewhere—anywhere—else. Both boys asked their father if they could return home and attend Campbell College in Belfast. Albert wanted the boys to stay at the school in Great Britain so they could learn how to be proper gentlemen.

In 1910, Jack **transferred** to Campbell College. He developed **respiratory** problems and had to leave the school. He then went to another school called Cherbourg. Cherbourg was in the town of Malvern, England, where Warren was living. Although Jack and Warren did not attend the same school, the two brothers were happy to live in the same town again.

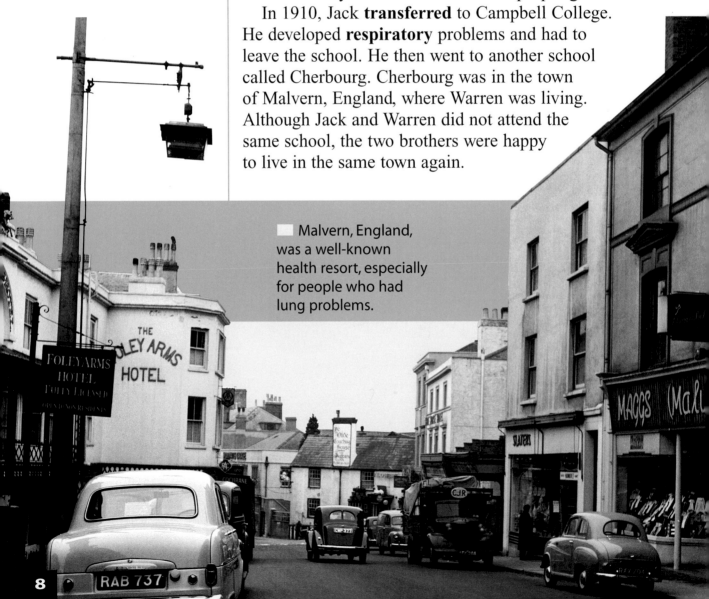

Malvern, England, was a well-known health resort, especially for people who had lung problems.

Jack caused trouble at Cherbourg, especially when he spent time with his older brother. Jack broke school rules and was punished with detentions and extra work.

Although Jack was **mischievous**, he was a good student. At Cherbourg, Jack studied Latin and English. He also wrote stories. In 1912, while he was at home on vacation, Jack wrote a story called "Boxen," or "Scenes from Boxonian City Life." It was based on the stories that he and Warren had made up when they were younger.

Even with so many stories in his head, Jack often felt lonely. He liked to read and became very **absorbed** in books. He worried about what other people might think of him. The only person he told about the things happening in his imagination was Warren.

Inspired to Write

Jack said that when he was writing, he saw pictures in his head before he knew what the story would be about. The pictures had a common "smell" and "flavor." If he waited for a while, the pictures connected into a story.

Jack's mother and governess taught him to read. Most children learn to read books in the first grade.

In 1916, at the age of 18, Jack wrote the entrance exams for Oxford University. He did so well on his exams that the school offered him a **scholarship**. Jack attended classes from April until September. At the same time, World War I was being fought. Jack decided that studying at Oxford had to wait.

Jack joined the British army and fought in the war. He arrived in France in November 1917. Jack was very **modest** about how he helped in the war. At one point, he captured a group of enemy soldiers. Still, he did not talk about these events.

On April 15, 1918, Jack was wounded in the Battle of Arras. Warren, who was also in France, travelled 50 miles (80 kilometers) on a bicycle to see Jack. Jack spent many months recovering. He returned to duty in October. He was assigned to Ludgerhall in Andover, England.

Oxford is the oldest English-speaking university. Jack earned two degrees studying at the school.

Jack was discharged from duty in December, 1918, after the war ended. In January, 1919, he returned to Oxford University. A collection of Jack's poems, called *Spirits in Bondage*, was published the same year.

Four years later, Jack graduated from Oxford with first-class honors in Greek and Latin Literature, Philosophy and Ancient History, and English Literature. He earned two degrees—one in **Classics** and one in English.

After graduation, Jack stayed at Oxford, working as a tutor. In 1925, he began teaching at Magdalen College at Oxford. There, he met John Tolkien. Both men were interested in science fiction and fantasy stories. In the 1930s, they encouraged each other to begin writing. Tolkien wrote a book about time travel. Jack wrote a story about space travel called *Out of the Silent Planet*.

John Tolkien met C. S. Lewis at Oxford University. Tolkien wrote The Lord of the Rings series.

Favorite Authors

Growing up, Jack loved books by Beatrix Potter. His favorite was *Squirrel Nutkin*. The book is about a naughty squirrel named Nutkin. Nutkin likes teasing a dangerous owl named Mr. Brown. Surprising events teach Nutkin to respect the owl. Other books that Jack enjoyed were *Gulliver's Travels*, *King Solomon's Mines*, and *Alice in Wonderland*. He also liked reading books by Mark Twain. The books Jack loved as a child helped shape his imagination so that he could become a writer.

Learning the Craft

When Jack was a boy, he sat in the wardrobe with his brother Warren, creating stories. Jack especially liked telling stories about animals that could talk.

In 1906, Jack wrote a play about Animal Land called *The King's Ring*. The characters included Sir Big, a frog **field marshal**; Mr. Ichthus-oress, a harp player; and— Jack's favorite—a brave knight named Sir Peter Mouse.

Jack wrote many stories about Peter Mouse. Peter Mouse lived in Mouse Land, which was ruled by an evil king named King Bublish. Mouse Land was one province, or area, in Animal Land. The other provinces were Pig Land, Squirrel Land, Fox Land, and Cat Land. In one adventure, Jack wrote about Peter Mouse leading the armies of Mouse Land into a battle with the cats of Cat Land. Many characters from these early stories can be found in Jack's later books.

The brave little mouse of Narnia, Reepicheep, may be based on Animal Land's Sir Peter Mouse.

When Jack began writing, he had no children of his own. In 1939, Great Britain was fighting in World War II. Children living in London were sent to homes in the country so they would be safe from bombings. Some of the **evacuees** came to live with Jack and Warren.

Jack and Warren had an old wardrobe that their father had built. One day, one of the little girls visiting asked Jack if there was anything behind the wardrobe. Jack remembered a story he had read called "The Aunt and Amabel." It was about a magical world behind a wardrobe.

Jack thought this might make a good idea for a book. In a notebook, he wrote a few sentences about four children named Ann, Martin, Rose, and Peter. These children had left London to live with a professor in the country because of bombings in London. Still, it was nine years before Jack began writing the first Narnia book, *The Lion, the Witch and the Wardrobe.*

Inspired to Write

Jack told people that *The Lion, the Witch and the Wardrobe* began with just one idea: a fawn carrying packages in a snowy wood. He was not sure what would happen next, until Aslan, the lion, bounded onto the scene. Jack said it was Aslan who brought all the stories together.

More than three million people, mostly children, were evacuated from British cities before World War II began. Most children went to the countryside. Jack thought that the best way to entertain the evacuees living with him was to tell them stories.

Getting Published

> "You are never too old to set another goal or to dream a new dream."
>
> C. S. Lewis

Long before Jack wrote the Narnia books, he wrote books for adults. As a teacher at Oxford, Jack continued to write. In 1938, Jack's first science-fiction book was published. It was called *Out of the Silent Planet*. The book was about three men who traveled to Mars. This story was followed by two more science-fiction books, *Perelandra* and *That Hideous Strength*.

Jack received many letters from fans of his science-fiction books. Several teachers at Oxford did not like the type of popular fiction that Jack was writing. They thought that he should write about more serious subjects. In 1935, after an Oxford professor's suggestion, Jack wrote the volume of sixteenth century English Literature for the Oxford History of English series. The volume, published in 1954, became an instant classic.

The Publishing Process

Publishing companies receive hundreds of **manuscripts** from authors each year. Only a few manuscripts become books. Publishers must be sure that a manuscript will sell many copies. As a result, publishers reject most of the manuscripts they receive.

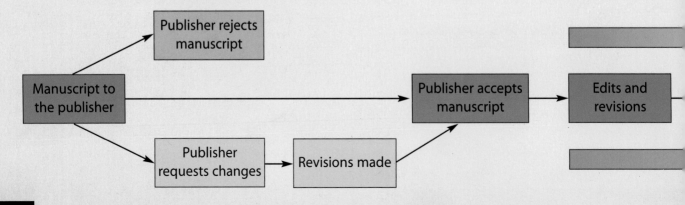

- Publisher rejects manuscript
- Manuscript to the publisher
- Publisher requests changes
- Revisions made
- Publisher accepts manuscript
- Edits and revisions

Jack finished writing *The Lion, the Witch and the Wardrobe* in 1949. He took it to his friend John Tolkien, but Tolkien did not like it. He thought Jack had written the book too quickly. Jack was shocked. He was sure it was good, so he took the book to a publisher, Geoffrey Bles. Bles liked it and told Jack to write more books about the land called Narnia.

When *The Lion, the Witch and the Wardrobe* was published in 1950, it received mixed **reviews**. Some people loved the book, while others hated it. Many parents and adults thought that the book was too scary for children. At first, the book did not sell well. Still, children loved it. The book soon became very popular.

After the final book in the series, *The Last Battle*, was published, Jack received the 1956 Carnegie Medal. The award recognizes an outstanding book published in the United Kingdom.

Inspired to Write

Like many authors, Jack wrote about what he knew. In *The Lion, the Witch and the Wardrobe*, the children explore indoors because it is raining. As a child, Jack often could not go outside because of rain. In *The Magician's Nephew*, a character tries to help his ill mother. This is similar to Jack's own experience as a boy.

Once a manuscript has been accepted, it goes through many stages before it is published. Often, authors change their work to follow an editor's suggestions. Once the book is published, some authors receive royalties. This is money based on book sales.

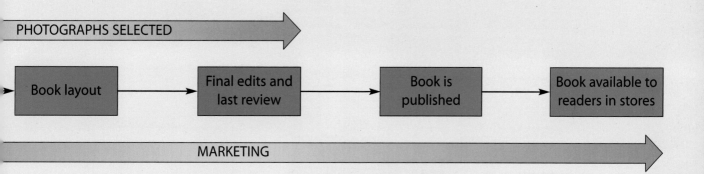

PHOTOGRAPHS SELECTED

Book layout → Final edits and last review → Book is published → Book available to readers in stores

MARKETING

Writer Today

During World War II, C. S. Lewis began speaking on radio programs. He usually spoke about **Christianity**. In 1952, Jack met an American writer named Joy Greshem. Jack and Joy shared many interests.

Jack and Joy married in 1956. Their marriage was short but happy. In 1956, Joy discovered that she had bone cancer. In 1957, she began to get better, and her family, friends, and doctors thought that she would **recover**. Sadly, in 1960, the cancer returned. Joy died in the hospital with Jack by her side. Jack was very sad about Joy's death. He did what he loved to do— he wrote about it. The book he wrote was called *A Grief Observed*. He hoped it would help other people who had lost people they loved.

■ During his career, Jack wrote about forty books. Only seven of these were written for children.

In 1961, Jack became ill. He had kidney and heart problems. Even though he was sick, Jack continued to work at Oxford University. He died on November 22, 1963. It was the same day that President John F. Kennedy was assassinated.

The stories from Jack's imagination still exist in his books. Over the years, The Chronicles of Narnia series has grown more popular. They are some of the most popular children's books that have ever been written. Many people have written about C. S. Lewis and the Narnia books. There are C. S. Lewis societies throughout the world. Society members discuss C. S. Lewis, his life, and his books.

In 2003, a play based on the book, *The Lion, the Witch and the Wardrobe,* was performed in Sydney, Australia.

Popular Books

C.S. Lewis is best known for the popular Narnia books. At the center of all the books is Aslan, the great lion. The following are brief descriptions from some of these stories.

C. S. Lewis

The Magician's Nephew

Book 6 in the Chronicles of Narnia

The Magician's Nephew

This book was written after *The Lion, the Witch and the Wardrobe*, even though it takes place before *The Lion, the Witch and the Wardrobe*. Jack wrote this book to explain why there was a wardrobe and how Aslan created Narnia. Digory Kirke and his friend Polly are the main characters in the book.

Digory's uncle is a magician who tricks Digory and Polly into traveling to Narnia. After many adventures, Digory and Polly watch Aslan create Narnia. Then, Aslan gives the children a magic apple and helps them return home. Digory plants the apple core in his yard, and a magical tree grows. He uses the tree to build the wardrobe.

The Lion, the Witch and the Wardrobe

The best known of The Chronicles of Narnia is about four children—Peter, Susan, Edmund, and Lucy. They are sent to live in the country with their uncle, Digory Kirke, because of the war. On the first day, Lucy climbs into a wardrobe and goes through the other side into a magical world called Narnia. The White Witch has put a spell on Narnia so that it is always winter, but never Christmas. Lucy goes back to Narnia through the wardrobe to tell the others about what she has seen. They do not believe her. The other children enter the wardrobe and arrive in Narnia with Lucy. They meet Aslan, a lion, who protects them from the White Witch and helps them save Narnia from eternal darkness.

The Voyage of the Dawn Treader

Another year has passed since the children were in Narnia. In Narnia, 3 years have passed. Edmund and Lucy spend the holidays with their cousin, Eustace Scrub, who likes to make fun of their stories about Narnia. On the wall of Lucy's bedroom is a picture of a ship from Narnia. One day, when all the children are in her room, the ship begins to move, and they are all pulled into the picture. Eustace is very unhappy, but the other children are happy to see their old friends again. Prince Caspian is now king. He tells the children that he is looking for seven royal lords who were sent away many years before. While helping King Caspian look for the missing lords, the children are captured by slave traders and attacked by a sea serpent. Eustace learns a hard lesson when he is changed into a terrible dragon. In the end, they all return home, although Aslan tells Edmund and Lucy they will not be able to return to Narnia.

The Silver Chair

Chased by bullies, Eustace and his friend Jill pass through a door to another world. In Narnia, Eustace finds that more than 70 years have passed, even though it only seems like a few weeks. Aslan tells Eustace and Jill that they need to find Prince Rilian, King Caspian's only son. King Caspian is an old man who is close to death. When he dies, there will be no one to take his place as King of Narnia. Aslan gives the children four signs to help them on their important journey. The signs are difficult to see. Sometimes the children miss the signs and get into trouble. They meet giants and a witch, who changes into a dangerous serpent. Finally, Eustace and Jill find Prince Rilian and return home.

The Last Battle

The Last Battle is the final book in The Chronicles of Narnia. Aslan brings Eustace and Jill back to the magical world to help him defend the country in an important battle against evil. The year is 2555. A donkey named Puzzle has disguised himself as Aslan and has sold all the creatures in Narnia as slaves for the cruel Calormenes. Everyone in Narnia believes it was really Aslan who turned against them. They are afraid. Eustace and Jill fight with King Tirian in the Last Battle.

AWARDS
The Last Battle
1956 Carnegie Medal

Creative Writing Tips

There is no correct way to write a book. Some writers create their most famous works when they are young. Others, like Jack Lewis, wait until they are older. When he was a boy, Jack kept a journal. He wrote poems, stories, and notes for future books.

Create Your Own Characters

When Jack was a child, he wrote stories about Animal Land. His stories included drawings of some of the characters and maps of where everything was located in Animal Land. The Narnia stories developed from Animal Land. Do you have an idea for a story? Think about where it will take place and who will be in it.

Read as Much as Possible

Authors get some of their ideas from books that they read. As a boy, Jack read as much as he could. He liked books about animals that could talk and fantasy stories about magical places. When Jack wrote the Narnia stories, his stories were **influenced** by some of the books he loved best.

In Jack's early story "Boxen," a rabbit ruled the land.

Take Notes

Many authors do not think of all the ideas for a book at one time. They might think of a funny character one day and a whole **scene** the next. It may take a long time for all the pieces to come together into a book. During World War II, Jack scribbled down a couple of sentences about four children who stayed in the country because of the war. This was the beginning of *The Lion, the Witch and the Wardrobe*.

Keep a Journal

Keeping a journal will help you practice your writing. The more you write, the better you will become. When Jack was 8 years old, he began to write in a diary. Sometimes he wrote about boring things. From 1922 to 1927, Jack wrote about taking care of chickens, washing dishes, and sawing wood.

Write and Rewrite

Many books are rewritten many times. John Tolkien did not like the first version of *The Lion, the Witch and the Wardrobe*. Jack was discouraged. He put the book away for some time. Then, he rewrote the first few chapters into a second **draft**.

Inspired to Write

While he was at Oxford, Jack started a writing club with his friend John Tolkien and some other writers. It was called The Inklings. The Inklings met once each week. They talked about what they were writing and read to the others what they had written that week. It was helpful for Jack to hear what other people thought of his stories.

C. S. Lewis was not the only member of his family to keep a diary. His brother, Warren, and his father also kept diaries.

Writing a Biography Review

A biography is an account of an individual's life that is written by another person. Some people's lives are very interesting. In school, you may be asked to write a biography review. The first thing to do when writing a biography review is to decide whom you would like to learn about. Your school library or community library will have a large selection of biographies from which to choose.

Are you interested in an author, a sports figure, an inventor, a movie star, or a president? Finding the right book is your first task. Whether you choose to write your review on a biography of C. S. Lewis or another person, the task will be similar.

Begin your review by writing the title of the book, the author, and the person featured in the book. Then, start writing about the main events in the person's life. Include such things as where the person grew up and what his or her childhood was like. You will want to add details about the person's adult life, such as whether he or she married or had children. Next, write about what you think makes this person special. What kinds of experiences influenced this individual? For instance, did he or she grow up in unusual circumstances? Was the person determined to accomplish a goal? Include any details that surprised you.

A concept web is a useful research tool. Use the concept web on the right to begin researching your biography review.

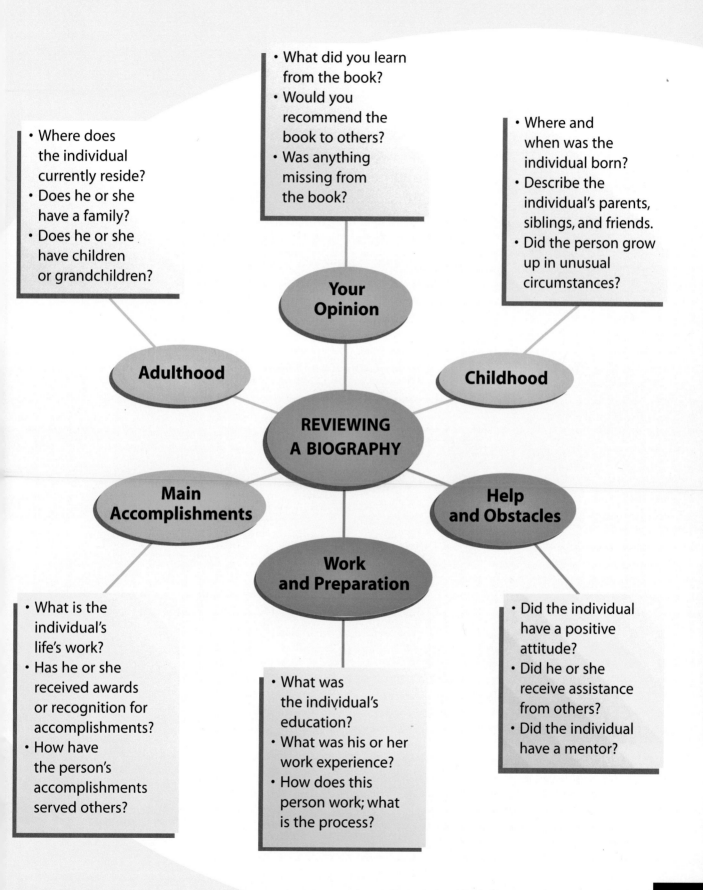

- Where does the individual currently reside?
- Does he or she have a family?
- Does he or she have children or grandchildren?

- What did you learn from the book?
- Would you recommend the book to others?
- Was anything missing from the book?

- Where and when was the individual born?
- Describe the individual's parents, siblings, and friends.
- Did the person grow up in unusual circumstances?

Your Opinion

Adulthood

Childhood

REVIEWING A BIOGRAPHY

Main Accomplishments

Help and Obstacles

Work and Preparation

- What is the individual's life's work?
- Has he or she received awards or recognition for accomplishments?
- How have the person's accomplishments served others?

- What was the individual's education?
- What was his or her work experience?
- How does this person work; what is the process?

- Did the individual have a positive attitude?
- Did he or she receive assistance from others?
- Did the individual have a mentor?

Fan Information

Children still love The Chronicles of Narnia. Jack received thousands of fan letters while he was alive. Children also sent him their own stories and poems. Although Jack was very busy, he replied to all of the letters with help from his brother, Warren. After *The Last Battle* was published, many children wrote to Jack begging him to write more Narnia books. However, Jack knew the series was finished after the seventh book.

NARNIA

THE CHRONICLES   DISCOVER NARNIA   THE MOVIE

THE 7 BOOKS
Illustrated Narnia

C.S. LEWIS
The Creation of Narnia

EDITIONS

The 7 Books

THE MAGICIAN'S NEPHEW

Digory and Polly discover a secret passage that links their houses, and are tricked into vanishing out of this world and into the World of Charn, where they wake up the evil Queen Jadis. There, they witness the creation of the Land of Narnia, as it is sung into being by the Great Lion, Aslan.

English Years: 1900
Narnian Years: 1

Tell me more!   Read a chapter: ◈ HTML ◈ PDF

THE LION, THE WITCH, AND THE WARDROBE

Peter, Susan, Edmund, and Lucy find their way through an old wardrobe into the world of Narnia. There, they unite with Aslan to fight the White Witch and save Narnia from perpetual Darkness.

English Years: 1940
Narnian Years: 1000

Tell me more!   Read a chapter: ◈ HTML ◈ PDF

THE HORSE AND HIS BOY

Shasta escapes from the land of Calormen with a Narnian warhorse, Bree. Along with Aravis and her horse Hwin, they uncover a Calormene plot to conquer Narnia and must find a way to save Narnia and its people.

English Years: 1940
Narnian Years: 1014

Tell me more!   Read a chapter: ◈ HTML ◈ PDF

PRINCE CASPIAN

Troubled times have come to Narnia as it is gripped by civil war. Prince Caspian is forced to blow The Great Horn of Narnia

Jack received letters from adults, too. Joy Greshem wrote to Jack. Jack and Joy wrote letters back and forth for a couple of years, until she went to Great Britain to visit him. Joy's sons, Douglas and David, also loved the Narnia books. Jack and Joy married the same year *The Last Battle* was published. Television movies based on the books can be watched today. The first full-length movie version of *The Chronicles of Narnia: The Lion, the Witch and the Wardrobe* was released in 2005.

WEB LINKS

The Official Harper-Collins Web Site on C.S. Lewis

www.harperchildrens.com/hch/narnia

This Web site celebrates 50 years of The Chronicles of Narnia. You can learn more about C. S. Lewis and how he created Narnia.

The Narnia Web Site

www.narnia.com

This Web site explores the land of Narnia. You can also find information on the books and the movie.

Quiz

Q: Where was C. S. (Jack) Lewis born?

1

A: Belfast, Northern Ireland

Q: How many brothers and sisters did Jack have?

2

A: Jack had one brother, Warren.

Q: Where did Jack and Warren like to sit and tell each other stories?

3

A: In the wardrobe in the attic

Q: What was Jack's favorite book as a child?

A: *Squirrel Nutkin* by Beatrix Potter

Q: Which war did Jack fight in?

A: World War I

Q: At which university did Jack teach?

A: Oxford University

Q: What was the name of the first book that Jack wrote in The Chronicles of Narnia series?

A: *The Lion, the Witch and the Wardrobe*

Q: Which of Jack's books won a Dale Carnegie Award?

A: *The Last Battle*

Q: What famous writer was Jack's friend?

A: J. R. R. (John) Tolkien

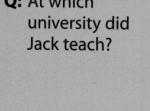

Q: Who did Jack marry?

A: Joy Gresham

Writing Terms

This glossary will introduce you to some of the main terms in the field of writing. Understanding these common writing terms will allow you to discuss your ideas about books and writing with others.

action: the moving events of a work of fiction

antagonist: the person in the story who opposes the main character

autobiography: a history of a person's life written by that person

biography: a written account of another person's life

character: a person in a story, poem, or play

climax: the most exciting moment or turning point in a story

episode: a short piece of action, or scene, in a story

fiction: stories about characters and events that are not real

foreshadow: hinting at something that is going to happen later in the book

imagery: a written description of a thing or idea that brings an image to mind

narrator: the speaker of the story who relates the events

nonfiction: writing that deals with real people and events

novel: published writing of considerable length that portrays characters within a story

plot: the order of events in a work of fiction

protagonist: the leading character of a story; often a likable character

resolution: the end of the story, when the conflict is settled

scene: a single episode in a story

setting: the place and time in which a work of fiction occurs

theme: an idea that runs throughout a work of fiction

Glossary

absorbed: to only pay attention to one thing

Christianity: members of religious group who practice the teachings of Jesus Christ

cisterns: containers that hold water or other liquids

Classics: literature of lasting significance

draft: a rough copy of something written

evacuees: people who must leave a place to avoid war or disaster

field marshal: the highest-ranking officer in the British army

governess: a woman who cares for and teaches children in their home

influenced: affected by the ideas of others

manuscripts: drafts of stories before they are published

mischievous: playful but troublesome

modest: humble

mythical: imaginary

recover: to become well again

respiratory: related to breathing

reviews: opinions written about a book

scene: a single episode in a story

scholarship: a financial award to attend school; often pays the studying, or tuition, fees

transferred: moved from one place to another

wardrobe: a closet or cabinet in which clothes are hung

Index

Photo Credits

Cover: John Chillingworth/Picture Post/Getty Images
Corbis: page 10; Getty Images: pages 1 (Hans Wild/Time Life Pictures), 3 (John Chillingworth), 4 (John Chillingworth/Picture Post), 7 (Taxi), 8 (Harry Kerr/BIPs), 9 (Stockbyte Platinum), 11 (Time Life Pictures/TimePix), 13 (Fox Photos), 16 (John Chillingworth), 17 (Patrick Riviere), 22 (Taxi), 23 (Imagebank), 26 (Imagebank), 28 (John Chillingworth/Picture Post); courtesy of HarperCollins Publishers: pages 12, 18, 19, 20, 21.